You said it, Shakespeare!

You said it, Shakespeare!

by

William Garvin

Paul S. Eriksson, Inc.
New York

Published simultaneously in the Dominion of Canada by Fitzhenry & Whiteside, Ltd., Ontario. Library of Congress Catalog Card Number 72-76291. Standard Book Number 8397-8700-6. Manufactured in the United States of America.

To Natalie

Contents

Prologue

This is not a textbook. Be assured (or warned) of that at once. It is, instead, a comic exercise in what could perhaps be called Literary Time Travel—an attempt to bridge the gap between Shakespeare's day and our own; and the purpose is strictly entertainment, not instruction. To be specific, this book contains a selection of authentic Shakespearean quotations that have been applied with satiric intent to the 20th Century . . . just as if the Bard of Avon were wryly commenting on us, and our way of life, today.

The works of William Shakespeare might seem to be an improbable subject for a humor book, but the notion is not really as odd as it first appears. Gentle Will was, as well as being many other things, a man of wit. He appreciated a good jest. He dealt with dialect humor and situation comedy on occasion. He was not above using even humor's so-called lowest form: the pun. And he conceived a sizable gallery of comic, grotesque or downright ludicrous characters. Of course, we cannot tell how he would have reacted to the idea of having many of his lines quoted out of context, even in fun; but I do have a feeling that the creator of Jack Falstaff could not have objected.

A brief explanation of my methods might be in order. They are, hopefully, in the scholarly tradition. Every quotation is exact and correct. Not a comma is out of place, not a capital letter changed. If irrelevant matter was removed, I have so indicated by using the customary "leaders" (. . .); and if an "enabling word" or letter had to be added, the new material appears within parentheses. Each quotation is identified as to source—not merely the act and scene but the line as well. (Example: *Macbeth, V, 3, 40.* This means that the passage quoted comes from Act 5, Scene 3 and Line 40 of *Macbeth.*) In short, I have taken no liberties with the Shakespearean text except to transport certain parts of it to our present day.

My final source was the standard Oxford edition of *The Complete Works of William Shakespeare* (1944-45). Readers who wish to locate specific quotations in their original settings —and, incidentally, check on my accuracy—should note that there are many published editions of Shakespeare's works, some with slight variations in line numbers. A line I identify as 85 in the Oxford edition might be 82 or 87 in another book. It would be similarly helpful to keep in mind the fact that a number of published volumes of Shakespeare have arbitrary or inaccurate line numberings.

I am particularly indebted to the editors of *Look, Mad* and the Philadelphia *Sunday Bulletin Magazine* for permission to reprint some material which appeared in their pages in shorter form. I am also grateful to the kind and efficient ladies of the Ardmore (Pa.) Free Library for their helpfulness in supplying much-needed reference materials.

Finally, a special note of thanks to my unwitting collaborator, William Shakespeare, who provided the rich basic substance of this book while I served merely as a prompter. I can only hope that the results of our joint efforts will be amusing enough to warrant the reader's conclusion that, in Shakespeare's own words, *Though this be madness, yet there is method in't.*

Now it's time to let the Bard speak for himself.

WILLIAM GARVIN

You said it, Shakespeare!

TRAVEL POSTER

I rather would entreat thy company
To see the wonders of the world abroad
Than (live) dully sluggardiz'd at home . . .

—Two Gentlemen of Verona I, 1, 5

BUSY MOTEL

. . . for three months . . . No . . . vacancy, –
Both day and night . . .

—Twelfth-Night V, 1, *98*

PILOT TO HIJACKER

I charge thee . . . do not interrupt me in my course.

—Romeo and Juliet V, 3, 25

VISIT LAS VEGAS, WHERE . . .

Pleasure and action make the hours seem short.

—Othello II, 3, 388

OR HOW ABOUT MIAMI?

Come on . . . down . . .

—The Tempest II, 2, 166

DIRECTIONS (or "You Can't Get There From Here.")

Turn up on your right hand at the next turning, but, at the next turning of all, on your left; . . . at the very next turning, turn of no hand, but turn down indirectly . . .

—Merchant of Venice II, 2, 42

MIXUP IN THE HOTEL RESERVATION

You must foresake this room and go . . .

—Othello V, 2, 329

NATIVE RETURNS TO NEW ENGLAND FOR A REST

. . . I may quietly Enjoy mine own . . . Maine . . .
Free from oppression . . .

—1 Henry VI V, 3, 152

Travel

Therefore devise with me how we may fly,
Whither to go, and what to bear with us . . .

—*As You Like It* I, 3, 103

AIRLINE AD (Hard Sell)

'Fly, fly, fly!' Fly, my lord, fly.

—Julius Caesar V, 5, 43

NO, GO BY RAILROAD

The . . . train (is) better worth than all . . .

—2 Henry VI I, 3, 88

NO, A SHIP IS BEST

(There is) no more delight
Than to be under sail and gone tonight.

—Merchant of Venice II, 6, *67*

THE HILTON HOTELS

Well, if we had of every nation a traveller, we should lodge them . . .

—Pericles IV, 2, 125

POSTCARD

. . . wish You . . . (were) here . . .

—Measure for Measure IV, 1, *12*

SOME PEOPLE LIKE SKI RESORTS

. . . but the many will be too chill and tender,
and they'll be for the . . . way that leads to . . .
the great fire.

—*All's Well That Ends Well IV*, 5, 57

OTHERS PREFER THE BEACH

. . . where, wretches, their poor bodies
Must lie and fester.

—*Henry V IV, 3, 87*

IT'S A NICE PLACE TO VISIT, BUT . . .

I would not there reside . . .

—*Othello I*, 3, *243*

SOAP OPERAS

If you have tears, prepare to shed them now.

—Julius Caesar III, 2, 174

CHANNEL- SWITCHING

Pray you, poor gentleman, take up some other station . . .

—Coriolanus IV, 5, 33

CRIME SHOWS

. . . how shall we stretch our eye
When capital crimes, chew'd,
swallow'd and digested,
Appear before us?

—Henry V II, 2, 55

MEDICAL SHOWS

If thou couldst, doctor . . . find her disease,
And purge it to a sound and pristine health,
I would applaud thee to the very echo . . .

—Macbeth V, 3, 50

EXERCISE SHOWS (for reducers)

O! that this too too solid flesh would melt . . .

—Hamlet I, 2, 129

"GET SMART" ("I find that hard to believe, Max.")

. . . would (you) believe that there were
mountaineers Dew-lapp'd like bulls . . . ?

—The Tempest III, 3, 44

NEWS

Thou hast made me giddy With these ill tidings.

—King John IV, 2, 132

WEATHER REPORT

. . . like a prophet suddenly enrapt
To tell thee that this day is ominous . . .

—Troilus and Cressida V, 3, 65

COMMERCIALS

'Zounds! I was never so bethump'd with words
Since I first call'd my brother's father dad.

—*King John II*, 1, *466*

LATE SHOW

Watch thou and wake when others be asleep . . .

—*2 Henry VI I*, 1, *250*

"AND NOW, HERE'S LAWRENCE WELK!"

. . . to give forth The corn . . .

—*Coriolanus III*, 1, *112*

THE REPAIRMAN'S VERDICT

I must take out the (whole) work!

—*Othello IV*, 1, *157*

Television

Out, damned spot! out, I say!

—Macbeth V, 1, *38*

Sports

NEW YORK METS BATTER

Hath all his ventures fail'd? What, not one hit?

–The Merchant of Venice III, 2, 268

UMPIRES

Thou blind fool . . . what dost thou to (thine) eyes,
That they behold, and see not what they see?

–Sonnet 137 Lines 1 and 2

Turn out that eyeless villain . . .

–King Lear III, 7, 96

WHERE DO THE DODGERS PLAY FIRST?

. . . the heavenly-harness'd team
Begins (its) golden progress in the east.

–1 Henry IV III, 1, 221

GOLF

. . . yet would I knew That stroke would prove the worst!

—Othello IV, 1, *285*

WRESTLING

. . . he would make you believe it was done in fight . . .

—1 Henry IV II, 4, *340*

POKER

Have I not here the best cards for the game
To win this easy match . . . ?

—King John V, 2, *105*

(LATER)

I ne'er had worse luck in my life . . .

—All's Well That Ends Well II, 2, *63*

FOOTBALL COACH'S INSTRUCTIONS

. . . not a man Shall pass (t)his quarter . . .

—Timon of Athens V, 4, *60*

I would give all my fame for a pot . . .

–Henry V III, 2, 14

STOP HIM GENTLY, MEN, GENTLY

. . . the silken tackle . . . with the touches of those flower-soft hands . . .

—Antony and Cleopatra II, 2, 217

THE TEAM CAPTAIN IS DISGUSTED

O! my offen(s)e is rank, it smells to heaven . . .

—Hamlet III, 3, 36

BOWLING (Heckling an Opponent)

Thou canst not hit it, hit it, hit it,
Thou canst not hit it, my good man.

—Love's Labour's Lost IV, 1, 129

HORSE RACING (A Day at the Track)

I must go with you to Belmont.

—The Merchant of Venice II, 2, 194

Five . . . to twenty! though the odds be great, I doubt not . . .

—3 Henry VI I, 2, 70

. . . use your legs, take the start, run . . .

—The Merchant of Venice II, 2, 6

Come on, come on, come on . . .

—2 Henry IV III, 2, 1

Why, one that rode to's execution . . .
Could never go so slow . . .

—Cymbeline III, 2, 70

A horse! a horse! my kingdom for a horse!
—Richard III V, 4, 13

Where's the fool now?
—Timon of Athens II, 2, 58

Last in the field . . .
—King John V, 5, 8

I have heard of riding wagers,
Where horses have been nimbler than the sands
That run i' the clock's behalf. But this is
foolery . . .
—Cymbeline III, 2, 72

I lost a couple . . . I lost—All mine own folly . . .
—Winter's Tale V, 1, 132 and 134

Come, come; no longer will I be a fool . . .
—Comedy of Errors II, 2, 207

THE TEEN-AGE BOY

And can you, by no drift of circumstance,
Get from him why he puts on this confusion,
Grating so harshly all his days . . .
With turbulent and dangerous lunacy?

—Hamlet III, 1, *1*

THE TEEN-AGE GIRL

O! what a scene of foolery have I seen,
Of sighs, of groans, of sorrow, and of teen . . .

—Love's Labour's Lost IV, 3, 163

TEEN PARTY

. . .'twas a din to fright a monster's ear,
To make an earthquake; sure it was the roar
Of a whole herd of lions.

—The Tempest II, 1, *321*

THE PARTY AT FULL BLAST

O! how this discord doth afflict my soul!

—1 Henry VI III, 1, *106*

FATHER, AFTER DAUGHTER HAS BEEN ON PHONE FOR AN HOUR

What! . . . have you not done talking yet?

—Troilus and Cressida III, 2, *107*

HAIR STYLES (BOYS)

Comb down his hair; look! look! it stands upright, Like lime-twigs . . .

—2 Henry VI III, 3, 15

TEEN SONG CRAZE

. . . 'tis no matter how it be in tune so it make noise enough.

—As You Like It IV, 2, *8*

THE BEATLES HAVE ARRIVED

. . . with strange . . . noises Of roaring, shrieking, howling . . .

—The Tempest V, 1, *232*

Why, then, your ladyship must cut your hair.
—*Two Gentlemen of Verona II*, 7, 44

TEEN SINGING
IDOL

Till each to . . . oblivion yield his part Of thee,
thy record never can be miss'd.

—Sonnet 122 Lines 7 and 8

SHOPPING FOR CLOTHES (DAUGHTER)

. . . the careful search . . . Is made with all due
diligence . . . and high expense . . .

—Pericles (Gower), III, 16

"BUT, DAD, I SIMPLY *MUST*
HAVE A BIGGER ALLOWANCE!"

There is money; spend it, spend it; spend more;
spend all I have . . .

—Merry Wives of Windsor II, 2, 245

APRIL 15th IS APPROACHING

There is some ill a-brewing . . .
For I did dream of money-bags to-night.

—The Merchant of Venice II, 5, *17*

READING THE INSTRUCTIONS

Good God! why should they mock poor fellows
thus?

—Henry V IV, 3, 92

LOOKING OVER FORM 1040

He apprehends a world of figures here,
But not the form . . .

—1 Henry IV I, 3, 209

SCHEDULES B, C, C-3, D, ETC.

Mis-shapen chaos of well-seeming forms!

—Romeo and Juliet I, 1, *184*

LISTING BUSINESS EXPENSES FOR UNCLE SAM:

What figure . . . think you he will bear?

—Measure for Measure I, 1, *16*

TOTAL TAX DUE

What is the gross sum that I owe . . . ?

—2 Henry IV II, 1, *94*

WRITING THE CHECK

O break, my heart!—poor bankrupt,
break at once!

—Romeo and Juliet III, 2, *57*

TAX AGENT EXAMINES THE RETURN:

. . . never saw I figures so likely to report . . .

—Cymbeline II, 4, *82*

EXCUSE FOR LATE FILING

Have I not told thee how I was cozened by the way, and lost all my money?

—The Winter's Tale IV, 3, 253

TAX CHEATER

. . . a crooked figure may Attest in . . . place (of) a million . . .

—Henry V (Prologue), 15

Rate me at what thou wilt, thou shalt be paid.

—2 Henry VI IV, 1, *30*

AUTO AD (STATUS APPROACH)

Wilt thou aspire to guide the heavenly car . . . ?

—Two Gentlemen of Verona III, 1, *154*

AUTO MAKER GOES AFTER MASS MARKET

He woos both high and low, both rich and poor,
Both young and old . . . Ford.

—Merry Wives of Windsor II, 1, *115*

DEALER TALKS TO PROSPECT

A time, methinks . . .
To make a world-without-end bargain in.

—Love's Labour's Lost V, 2, *796*

A PURCHASE THAT DIDN'T WORK OUT

A gilt nutmeg. A lemon. Stuck...

—Love's Labour's Lost V, 2, 649

TRAFFIC JAM

I can no further crawl, no further go...

—Midsummer-Night's Dream III, 2, 444

SLOWPOKE IN FRONT

...thou drone, thou snail, thou slug...!

—Comedy of Errors II, 2, 198

Traffic confound thee, if the gods will not!

—Timon of Athens I, 1, 245

He heareth not, he stirreth not, he moveth not;
(I think) The ape is dead...

—Romeo and Juliet II, 1, 15

CAR MAKER'S CREED

Then may I set the world on wheels, when she can spin for (my) living.

—Two Gentlemen of Verona III, 1, 320

WOMAN PARKING

...stand far off. Stand back! room! bear back!

—Julius Caesar III, 2, 172

WOMAN DRIVER

. . . to ride day and night; and not to deliberate, not to remember, not to have patience to shift . . .

—*2 Henry IV V*, 5, 22

DESIGNERS

What do we do then but draw anew the model . . . ?

—*2 Henry IV I*, 3, 46

TRYING TO START

If I begin the battery once again, I will . . . leave . . .

—*Henry V III*, 3, 7

You said it, Shakespeare!

THE ETERNAL FEMALE (MAN'S VIEWPOINT)

She works by charms, by spells, by the figure, and such daubery as this . . .

—*Merry Wives of Windsor IV*, 2, 189

ADVICE TO BEAUTICIAN

. . . let him not leave out The colour of her hair . . .

—*Antony and Cleopatra II*, 5, 113

WIFE'S LAMENT AT BREAKFAST

. . . thou hast spoken no word all this while.

—*Love's Labour's Lost V*, 1, 160

DIETER'S WISH

God keep lead out of me! I need no more weight . . .

—1 Henry IV V, 3, 35

COMPLIMENT FOR PARIS ORIGINAL

. . . your gown's a most rare fashion, i' faith.

—Much Ado About Nothing III, 4, 15

GIRL'S BEST FRIEND

Sir, I must have that diamond from you.

—Comedy of Errors V, 1, 394

NYLON HAZARD

Why do they run . . . ? this is a knavery of them to make me afeard.

—Midsummer-Night's Dream III, 1, 118

GOOD-LOOKING GIRL

The chief perfections of that lovely dame—
Had I sufficient skill to utter them—
Would make a volume of enticing lines . . .

—1 Henry VI V, 5, 12

WHY DO YOU WEAR PADDED BRAS, GIRLS?

. . . you must not think That we are made . . . so flat . . .

—Hamlet IV, 7, 30

MALE COMPLAINT

Canst thou not . . . Cleanse the stuff'd bosom of that perilous stuff Which weighs upon the heart?

—Macbeth V, 3, 40, 44

MOM, THE FAMILY MANAGER

. . . she has all the rule of her husband's purse . . .

—Merry Wives of Windsor I, 3, 56

There's language in her eye, her cheek, her lip,
Nay, (even) her foot speaks . . .

—*Troilus and Cressida IV*, 5, 55

ANY JOHN HUSTON FILM

. . . is altogether directed by an Irishman . . .

—Henry V III, 2, 73

ACTORS TO AGENT

. . . of all The treasure, in this field achiev'd . . .
We render you the tenth . . .

—Coriolanus I, 9, 32

TEN-PERCENTER'S LAMENT

O world! world! world! thus is the poor agent despised.

—Troilus and Cressida V, 10, 36

TALENT SCOUT'S REPORT

She sings like one immortal, and she dances
As goddess-like . . .

—Pericles (Gower), V, 3

HOLLYWOOD MUSICAL

. . . with a band of thirty thousand men . . .

–3 Henry VI II, 2, 68

THIRD-RATE COMEDIANS

. . . they have a plentiful lack of wit, together with most weak hams . . .

–Hamlet II, 2, 204

HOW TO LIST THE CREDITS

First . . . say what the play treats on; then read the names of the actors, and so grow to a point.

–Midsummer-Night's Dream I, 2, 8

REHEARSING A VAUDEVILLE ACT

Get your apparel together, good strings to your beards, new ribbons to your pumps; meet presently at the (P)alace; every man look o'er his part . . .

–Midsummer-Night's Dream IV, 2, 36

UNDERGROUND FILM

. . . a tale Told by an idiot, full of sound and fury, Signifying nothing.

–Macbeth V, 5, 26

PERSONAL APPEARANCE TOUR

... eat, speak, and move under the influence of the most received star ...

—*All's Well That Ends Well II,* 1, *55*

CONFIDENT MOVIE PRODUCER

I have set my life upon a cast,
And I will stand the hazard ...

—*Richard III V,* 4, *9*

BUT HE WANTS TOP STARS, ANYWAY—LIKE BURT

But as I come, I come for Lancaster.

—*Richard II II, 3, 114*

AND KIRK

... that sprightly ... Douglas ...

—*1 Henry IV II,* 4, *382*

THE DIRECTOR GIVES HIS INSTRUCTIONS

Speak the speech, I pray you ... trippingly on the tongue ... Nor do not saw the air too much with your hand ...

—*Hamlet III,* 2, *1 and 4*

THE FILM BEGINS

The actors are at hand; and, by their show,
You shall know all . . .

—Midsummer-Night's Dream V, 1, *116*

CRITIC'S COMMENT

A hit, a very palpable hit.

—Hamlet V, 2, *294*

FANS FLOCK TO BUY TICKETS

. . . give twenty, forty, fifty, a hundred ducats a-piece for his picture . . .

—Hamlet II, 2, *390*

PLEASED PRODUCER

Jove and my stars be praised!

—Twelfth-Night II, 5, *190*

"I NEED A DRINK!"

Any bar . . . will be medicinable to me . . .

—Much Ado About Nothing II, 2, 4

FRIENDLY TAVERN

. . . where, for one shot of five pence, thou shalt have five thousand welcomes.

—Two Gentlemen of Verona II, 5, 10

BARTENDER'S QUERY

What's your pleasure, sir?

—Antony and Cleopatra I, 2, 140

TIMID CUSTOMER'S REPLY

Doth it not show vilely in me to desire small beer?

—2 Henry IV II, 2, 7

"BUT PLEASE ADD . . ."

A piece of ice . . .

—Taming of the Shrew IV, 1, *14*

NEXT REQUEST

Go . . . fetch me a stoup of liquor.

—Hamlet V, 1, *66*

AND AFTER RECONSIDERING

. . . on the rocks . . .

—Pericles II, 1, 5

MUCH LATER

I have yet Room for six scotches more.

—Antony and Cleopatra IV, 7, *10*

"HOW IS YOUR DRINK, SIR?"

Not so hot . . .

—Winter's Tale II, 3, 32

I would your spirit(s) were . . . stronger . . . .

—Winter's Tale IV, 3, 518

SO BARTENDER ADDS...

Eye of newt, and toe of frog,
Wool of bat, and tongue of dog,
Adder's fork, and blind-worm's sting,
Lizard's leg, and howlet's wing . . .

—Macbeth IV, 1, 14

CUSTOMER TRIES IT AND COMMENTS

. . . ye gods, you make the weak most strong . . .

—Julius Caesar I, 3, 91

BARTENDER'S SUGGESTION (TWO HOURS LATER)

Go, go, you cot-quean, go;
Get you to bed; faith, you'll be sick tomorrow...

—Romeo and Juliet IV, 4, 6

BEFUDDLED PATRON'S EXCUSE

I cannot remember what I did when you made me drunk...

—Merry Wives of Windsor I, 1, 176

ANOTHER CUSTOMER'S COMMENT

... he feels no pain ...

—As You Like It III, 2, 343

BOUNCER'S COMMAND

Out, dog! out, cur! thou driv'st me past the bounds of maiden's patience.

—Midsummer-Night's Dream III, 2, 65

THE MORNING AFTER

... I was more than half stewed ...

—Merry Wives of Windsor III, 5, 124

Lord! how my head aches; what a head have I!
It beats as it would fall in twenty pieces.

—Romeo and Juliet II, 5, 49

SOLEMN PLEDGE

I'll ne'er be drunk whilst I live again ... honest ...

—Merry Wives of Windsor I, 1, 187

THE MAYOR

. . . he is himself alone, To answer all the city.

—Coriolanus I, 4, *50*

CHAMPS ÉLYSÉES (Paris)

This is a most majestic vision . . .

—The Tempest IV, I, *118*

URBAN RENEWAL PROJECTS

To unbuild the city and to lay all flat.

—Coriolanus III, 1, *197*

THE FREEWAY AT 5 P.M.

God for his mercy! what a tide . . .
Comes rushing on this woeful (road) at once!

—Richard II II, 2, 98

PHILADELPHIA, THE BUTT OF SOME JOKES

. . . to hear the city
Abus'd extremely, and to cry, 'That's witty!'

—Henry VIII (Epilogue), 5

SHUBERT ALLEY (New York):

Here the street is narrow: The throng that follows . . .
Will crowd a feeble man almost to death . . .

—Julius Caesar II, 4, 33

PARK AVENUE SET

Their spirits are so married in conjunction with the participation of society that they flock together . . .

—2 Henry IV V, 1, 76

TIMES SQUARE, THE LOOP, BETSY ROSS HOUSE, THE CAPITOL, ETC.

I pray you, let us satisfy our eyes
With the memorials and the things of fame
That do renown this city.

—Twelfth-Night III, 3, 22

YOUR HOME TOWN (THE CHAMBER OF COMMERCE VIEW)

This other Eden, demi-paradise . . .
This happy breed of men, this little world,
This precious stone set in the silver sea . . .
This blessed plot, this earth, this realm . . .

—*Richard II II*, 1, *42*

Politics

DEMOCRATIC CONVENTION (1968)

Hubert shall be your man . . .

—King John III, 3, 72

THE CAMPAIGN

Com'st thou with deep premeditated lines,
With written pamphlets studiously devis'd,
Humphrey . . . ?

—1 Henry VI III, 1, 1

WELL-KNOWN STATESMAN LOOKING FOR HIS WIFE

What, lamb! what, lady-bird! . . . where's this girl?

—Romeo and Juliet I, 3, 3

CONGRESSMAN TO PICKETERS

What! urge you your petitions in the street?
Come to the Capitol.

—Julius Caesar III, 1, *12*

SENATOR SPEAKS OUT AGAINST FOREIGN AID

Wilt thou, after the expense of so much money, be now a gainer?

—Merry Wives of Windsor II, 2, *148*

POLITICIAN'S VOTE-GETTING TECHNIQUE

. . . I can smooth and fill his . . . ear
With golden promises . . .

—Titus Andronicus IV, 4, *95*

VOTER'S REACTION TO CAMPAIGN SPEECH

These are but wild and whirling words, my lord.

—Hamlet I, 5, *133*

DIPLOMAT'S VIEW OF DE GAULLE

. . . Charles . . . is the stubbornest . . . fellow of France . . .

—As You Like It I, 1, *150*

KOSYGIN EXPLAINS STRATEGY TO THE POLITBURO

Then walk we forth . . .
And waving our red weapons o'er our heads,
Let's all cry, 'Peace . . . !'

—*Julius Caesar III*, 1, *108*

BARRY GOLDWATER MAKES PROMISE TO NELSON ROCKEFELLER
(keeping his fingers crossed)

I will become as liberal as you . . .

—*Merchant of Venice V*, 1, *226*

SUSPICIOUS ENVOY'S REPORT

Something is rotten in the state of Denmark.

—*Hamlet I*, 4, *90*

PRESIDENTIAL ASPIRANT'S RECURRING WISH

I will look again . . . for the nomination of the
party . . .

—*Love's Labour's Lost IV*, 2, *138*

PRESIDENT'S ADVICE TO SPIRO AGNEW

Seal up the mouth of outrage for a while . . .

—*Romeo and Juliet V*, 3, *216*

LYNDON WHO?

I cannot tell what the dickens his name is . . .
—Merry Wives of Windsor III, 2, 19

FAREWELL TO A GOOD LOSER

By heaven, Hubert, I am almost asham'd
To say what good respect I have of thee.
—King John III, 3, 27

Advertising

HIGH-LEVEL TRICKERY IN AN AGENCY

O my good lord!
At many times I brought in my accounts,
Laid them before you; you would throw them off,
And say you found them . . .

—*Timon of Athens II*, 2, *142*

AIR-CONDITIONER COMMERCIAL

. . . thou shalt soon feel . . . cold comfort . . . in thy hot office (!)

—*Taming of the Shrew IV*, 1, *33*

URGING CLIENT TO CONTINUE RUNNING THE AD

Thou shouldst print more, nor let that copy die.

—*Sonnet 11 Line 14*

MAN IN RENT-A-CAR COMMERCIAL

...vaulted with such ease into his seat,
As if an angel dropp'd down from the clouds...

—1 Henry IV IV, 1, *107*

DIRECT-MAIL EXECUTIVE

I warrant, he hath a thousand of these letters, writ with blank space for different names...

—Merry Wives of Windsor II, 1, *76*

HARD-SELL COSMETIC AD

... too flaming a praise for a good complexion.

—Troilus and Cressida I, 2, *111*

CELEBRITIES' TESTIMONIALS

Our praises are our wages...

—Winter's Tale I, 2, *94*

PLANNING THE CAMPAIGN

We'll...commend what we intend to sell.

—Troilus and Cressida IV, 1, *78*

"PLAYBOY" PHOTOGRAPHER'S INSTRUCTIONS

Therefore lay bare your bosom.

—Merchant of Venice IV, 1, *252*

"WHAT DO YOU LIKE ABOUT WOMEN?" (A Girl-Watcher's Confession):

. . . I Will praise a hand, a foot, a face,
an eye, A gait, a state, a brow, a breast,
a waist, A leg, a limb . . .

—Love's Labour's Lost IV, 3, 184

TRANSSEXUAL'S DILEMMA

To be, or not to be: that is the question . . .

—Hamlet III, 1, *56*

VERBAL ADVANCE (with exploring hand)

I pray thee, let me feel . . .

—*Two Gentlemen of Verona III*, 1, *136*

ADVANCE REFUSED ("Take your hand away!")

. . . do thy best
To pluck this crawling serpent from my breast.

—*Midsummer-Night's Dream II*, 2, *145*

PROCURER'S SUGGESTION

What say you to a piece . . . ?

—*Taming of the Shrew IV, 3, 23*

LOOKING THEM OVER

We first survey . . . the model; And when we see the figure . . . Then must we rate the cost of the erection . . .

—*2 Henry IV I, 3, 42*

BRAGGART

Now come I . . . mark the moan she makes . . .

—*Two Gentlemen of Verona II, 3, 33*

Sex

From fairies and the tempters of the night
Guard me, beseech ye!

—Cymbeline II, 2, 9

STRAIGHT GAL

She . . . Never lack'd gold and yet went never gay . . .

—Othello II, 1, *148, 150*

HANKY-PANKY IN THE MAID'S ROOM

When a man's servant shall play . . . with him, look you, it goes hard . . .

—Two Gentlemen of Verona IV, 4, *1*

NAUGHTY PROPOSITION

If . . . I have enjoyed the dearest bodily part of your mistress, my ten thousand ducats are yours; . . . if I come off . . . my gold (is) yours . . .

—Cymbeline I, 4, *166*

GREENWICH VILLAGE POLICE RAID

Fairies, be gone, and be all ways away.

—Midsummer-Night's Dream IV, 1, *47*

RECOUNTING A SEDUCTION

(He) shook The bosom . . . enter'd me, Yea, with a splitting power . . . And press'd in . . .

—Henry VIII II, 4, *180*

"DID I CATCH SOMETHING, DOCTOR?"

No, madam, these are no venereal signs . . .

—Titus Andronicus II, 3, 37

TRICKED BY A CAD

O! . . . pregnant, pregnant! The drug he gave me, which he said was precious And cordial to me, have I not found it Murderous to the senses?

—Cymbeline IV, 2, 325

WHAT DO YOU THINK OF SEX?

Is it sport? I think it is; and doth affection breed it? I think it doth . . .

—Othello IV, 3, 100

. . . a smoke rais'd with the fume of sighs . . .
a fire sparkling in lovers' eyes . . .
What is it else? a madness most discreet,
A choking gall, and a preserving sweet.

—Romeo and Juliet I, 1, 196

TODAY'S YOUNG PEOPLE

Is this the generation of love? hot blood? hot thoughts, and hot deeds?

—Troilus and Cressida III, 1, *146*

WHAT ARE THEY DOING?

. . . call it, Love-in . . .

—Midsummer-Night's Dream II, 1, *168*

WHY DO THEY LOOK LIKE THAT?

Full of strange oaths, and bearded like the pard . . .

—As You Like It II, 7, 150

With amber bracelets, beads and all this knavery.

—Taming of the Shrew IV, 3, 58

. . . with stinking clothes that fretted in their own grease . . .

—Merry Wives of Windsor III, 5, 117

HIPPIES' OPINION OF SQUARES

A crew of patches, rude mechanicals,
That work for bread . . .

—Midsummer-Night's Dream III, 2, 9

COLLEGE REBEL'S CRY

I protest, the schoolmaster is exceeding fantastical . . .

—Love's Labour's Lost V, 2, 529

DEAN'S COMMENT

The lady doth protest too much, methinks.

—Hamlet III, 2, 242

MAYOR DALEY'S COMMENT

. . . your insolent retinue
Do hourly carp and quarrel, breaking forth
In rank and not-to-be-endured riots.

—King Lear I, 4, 224

You said it, Shakespeare!

The foul practice Hath turn'd (me) on . . .

—Hamlet V, 2, 331

DOCTOR'S SECRET WISH

. . . you shall pay your fees When you depart, and save your thanks.

—Winter's Tale I, 2, 53

AMERICAN MEDICAL ASSOCIATION'S WASHINGTON OFFICE

The doctor is well money'd, and his friends Potent at court . . .

—Merry Wives of Windsor IV, 4, 90

IN THE HANDS OF A QUACK

. . . so long, health!

—Troilus and Cressida IV, I, *15*

PROCTOLOGIST'S SPECIALTY

. . . it concerns me To look into the bottom . . .

—Measure for Measure I, 1, 78

HIS PATIENT'S COMPLAINT

. . . I (have) such a tender ass . . .

—Midsummer-Night's Dream IV, 1, *28*

PSYCHOANALYST'S QUERY

What was your dream, my lord? I pray you, tell me.

—Richard III I, 4, *8*

PATIENT TO PSYCHIATRIST

Sir, You speak a language that I understand not . . .

—Winter's Tale III, 2, *80*

INSTEAD OF USING CLICHÉS . . . :

Canst thou not minister to a mind diseas'd,
Pluck from the memory a rooted sorrow,
Raze out the written troubles of the brain . . . ?

—Macbeth V, 3, 40

QUACKS' CONSULTATION

. . . when we debate Our trivial difference loud, we do commit Murder in healing wounds . . .

—Antony and Cleopatra II, 2, *20*

URINALYSIS

Sirrah . . . what says the doctor to my water?

—2 Henry IV I, 2, 1

NURSE'S CHART

. . . your pains Are register'd where every day I turn The Leaf to read them.

—Macbeth I, 3, 150

"WHY ARE YOU BANKRUPT, SIR?"

. . . twelvemonth in a hospital.

—Love's Labour's Lost V, 2, 879

REQUEST TO BROKER

. . . set me i' the stocks, i' the common stocks . . .
—Merry Wives of Windsor IV, 5, 125

NEWSPAPER STOCK QUOTATIONS

What see you in those papers that you lose
So much complexion?
—Henry V II, 2, 72

BULLISH BROKER

Come buy of me, come; come buy; come buy . . .
—Winter's Tale IV, 3, 230

. . . it is the right . . . market.
—As You Like It III, 2, 105

BEAR

. . . I must tell you friendly in your ear,
Sell when you can; you are not for all markets.

—*As You Like It* III, 5, 59

TIRED OF MONEY-MAKING

Buck! I would I could wash myself of the buck!
Buck, buck, buck!

—*Merry Wives of Windsor* III, 3, 166

TRANSFERRING A SALESMAN

. . . turn thou no more
To seek a living in our territory.

—*As You Like It* III, 1, 8

CREDIT MANAGER

He must observe . . . The quality of persons . . .
And (every) check . . . That comes before his eye.

—*Twelfth-Night* III, 1, 70

LABOR TROUBLE AT THE PLANT

. . . since we have begun to strike,
We'll never leave, till we have hewn thee down . . .

—*3 Henry VI* II, 2, 167

BOARDS OF DIRECTORS

They answer, in a joint and corporate voice . . .

—Timon of Athens II, 2, *214*

UNFRIENDLY COMPETITOR

If there be devils, would I were a devil . . .
So I might have your company in hell . . .

—Titus Andronicus V, 1, *147*

WALL STREET JOURNAL

There are some shrewd contents in yon same paper . . .

—Merchant of Venice III, 2, *244*

WHEN, WHEN, WHEN WILL YOU DELIVER?

Tomorrow, and tomorrow, and tomorrow . . .

—Macbeth V, 5, *19*

DICTATING TO SECRETARY

Take this . . . letter . . .

—Merchant of Venice III, 4, 47

. . . dear Harry . . .

—2 Henry IV II, 3, 12

"THE LOAN-COMPANY MAN CALLED, SIR!"

He humbly prays your speedy payment.

—Timon of Athens II, 2, 28

ACCOUNTANTS GET OUT THE RED INK

O! we have made a vow to study . . . our books
. . . (and)
In leaden contemplation have found . . .
Such fiery numbers . . .

—Love's Labour's Lost IV, 3, 318-322

SO HOW'S BUSINESS?

. . . do not ask . . .

—King John V, 7, 41

The Arts

VENUS DE MILO'S PLEA

I bepray you, let me borrow my arms again.

—Love's Labour's Lost V, 2, 701

MONA LISA

Why dost thou smile so . . . ?

—Twelfth-Night III, 4, 37

ANDY WARHOL

. . . I shall . . . be . . . camp, and profits will accrue.

—Henry V II, 1, 117

OP ART EXHIBITION

Behold, distraction, frenzy, and amazement,
Like witless anticks, one another meet . . .

—*Troilus and Cressida* V, 3, 85

O heavens! what stuff is here?

—*Measure for Measure* III, 2, 5

One (who) painted thus, Would be interpreted a thing perplex'd . . .

—*Cymbeline* III, 4, 6

Give me to know How this foul rout began, who set it on; And he that is approv'd in this offence . . .

—*Othello* II, 3, 211

THE ARTIST STRIKES BACK

You blocks, you stones, you worse than senseless things!

—*Julius Caesar* I, 1, 39

"1812 OVERTURE" (Tchaikovsky):

. . . you shall hear A fearful battle render'd you in music . . .

—*Henry V* I, 1, 43

SECOND-RATE CONCERT ARTIST

. . . a poor player That struts and frets his hour upon the stage, And then is heard no more . . .

—*Macbeth* V, 5, 24

OPERA HATER

A plague upon this howling! they are louder than the weather . . .

—*The Tempest* I, 1, 41

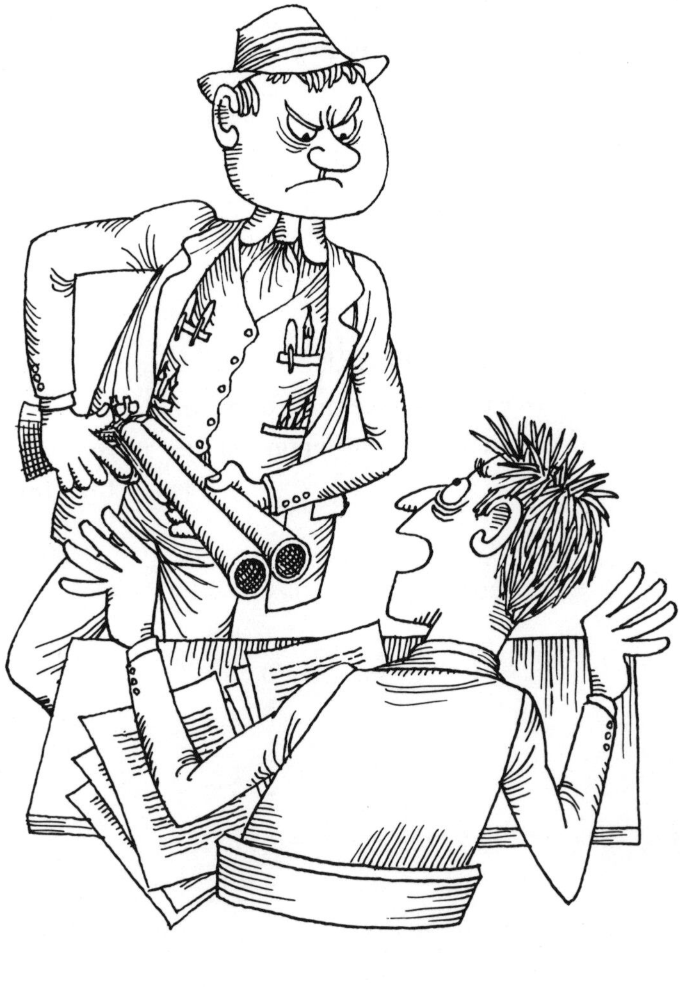

PUBLISHER TO AUTHOR

Seek you to . . . gripe (about) . . . The royalties . . . ?

—Richard II II, 1, *190*

FAR-OUT POET

I understand a fury in your words. But not the words.

—*Othello IV, 2, 31*

WILLIAM SHAKESPEARE

He was a man, take him for all in all,
(We) shall not look upon his like again.

—*Hamlet I, 2, 187*

JACK BENNY

Thou wilt fall backward when thou com'st to age...

–Romeo and Juliet I, 3, 56

MATTRESSES

We are such stuff As dreams are made on, and our little life Is rounded with a sleep.

–The Tempest IV, 1, *156*

BARGAIN BASEMENT CLEARANCE SALE

Let us . . . show our foulest wares,
And think perchance they'll sell . . .

–Troilus and Cressida I, 3, 359

WEARY WATCH REPAIRMAN

The time is out of joint; O cursed spite,
That ever I was born to set it right!

–Hamlet I, 5, *188*

NERVOUS WAITER

Tush! fear not, man, we'll tip . . . with gold . . .

–Much Ado About Nothing V, 4, *44*

GAMBLER'S QUERY

Where . . . is . . . (the) action (?)

–Pericles (Gower), 23

TOUGH COP

. . . this . . . sergeant . . . Is strict in his arrest . . .

–Hamlet V, 2, *350*

ARTHUR MURRAY, FRED ASTAIRE, ETC.

They bid us to the . . . dancing-schools . . .

–Henry V III, 5, *32*

SCIENCE-FICTION WRITER

I could a tale unfold whose lightest word
Would harrow up thy soul, freeze thy young blood,
Make thy two eyes, like stars, start from their spheres . . .

—*Hamlet I*, 5, 15

CARIBBEAN ENTERTAINERS

. . . some of 'em . . . Limbo . . . (which) they . . .
like to dance these days . . .

—*Henry VIII V*, 4, 69

ARMY INSPECTOR GENERAL

. . . I take my cause Out of the gripes of . . .
men . . .

—*Henry VIII V*, 3, 99

INTERNATIONAL SEAFOOD TYCOON

. . . the world's mine oyster . . .

—*Merry Wives of Windsor II*, 2, 2

THE ASTRONAUTS

Wilt thou reach stars . . . ?

—*Two Gentlemen of Verona III*, 1, 156

. . . I wash, wring, brew, bake, scour, dress meat and drink . . .

–Merry Wives of Windsor I, 4, 100

EINSTEIN'S THEORY

. . . those that understood him smiled at one another and shook their heads; but, for mine own part, it was Greek to me.

—Julius Caesar I, 2, 286

SLOW WAITERS

What service is here? I think our fellows are asleep.

—Coriolanus IV, 5, 1

CALLING THE REPAIRMAN

I do beseech you . . . To give me now a little benefit,
Out of those many register'd in promise . . . to come in my behalf.

—Troilus and Cressida III, 3, 13

COMPLAINING ABOUT HIS BILL

You charge me most unjustly.

—Othello IV, 2, 186

HEDONIST'S PHILOSOPHY

Live a little . . .

—As You Like It II, 6, 5

Epilogue

. . . shall that finish the jest?

—Love's Labour's Lost II, 1, *219*

There is no more . . . it is done . . .

—Richard III IV, 2, *79*

I pray . . . thou likest (it) . . .

—Much Ado About Nothing I, 1, *185*

finis